A GIFT FOR

_____

FROM

_____

YOUR Guardian Angel's GIFT

Christine K. Clifford

KPT PUBLISHING

Your Guardian Angel's Gift
Copyright © 2017 Christine K. Clifford

Published by KPT Publishing
Minneapolis, Minnesota 55406
www.KPTPublishing.com

ISBN 978-1-944833-15-2

Literary development and cover/interior design by
Koechel Peterson and Associates, Minneapolis, Minnesota.

First printing March 2017
10 9 8 7 6 5 4 3 2 1

Printed in the United States of America

Dedication

To Dan Ahlberg,

who has given me wings,

and to our family—

Ryan, Tim, Brady, Brooks, Chris,

Oksana, Katelyn and Kai—

who make us fly.

INTRODUCTION

Appropriately, it happened in the air.

I was on a flight. Appropriate, too, it was just before Christmas, when our thoughts so easily turn inward, and then upward.

I looked out the airplane window, reflecting on
a year of struggle and on how I'd overcome it.
And suddenly it came into view:

A feather,

I began to write. And I wrote and wrote and
wrote, and within seconds it seemed, it was
done: this poem, in the exact words that follow.

That moment was a gift to me.

This is mine to you.

—Christine K. Clifford

There's a story

to this feather

Rather simple

but it's true

It fell straight down from heaven

As a sign meant just for you.

See,
we all have lifelong
challenges,

Adversity and fear,

Your Guardian Angel's Gift

But your *Angel* up in

HEAVEN

Sees *every* little tear.

Your Guardian Angel's Gift

God
chose your
Special Angel

For those times you cannot

COPE.

He put Her there
to let you know,

Don't ever
give up *hope.*

If you struggle, fight,

or just feel lost,

You'll always know
She's there.

She sent this feather
down to earth

To let you know
"I Care."

If you ever feel you're

stumbling,

Remember: stand up
STRAIGHT AND TALL

Your Guardian Angel's Gift

Your personal Guardian Angel

Will never let you fall.

Your Guardian Angel's Gift

So if you're ever

FRIGHTENED,

WORRIED,

Lonely,

in DESPAIR

Remember
that this feather
traveled miles

through the air.

It went through
sleet
and rain and
and
snow,

Crossed deserts

far and wide.

It tossed about,

turned upside down

but landed by your side

It will always be
beside you,

A beacon

in the night,

And every morn as *daybreak comes,*

This gift will be *your light.*

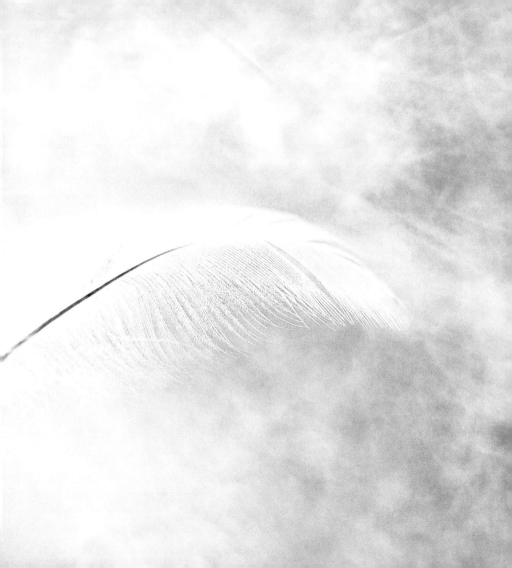

Before her first bout with breast cancer, Christine Clifford had definitely cracked the glass ceiling. At the age of forty, she was senior vice president for SPAR Marketing Services, an international information and merchandising services firm in Minneapolis, Minnesota

Now a two-time survivor, Christine has written nine books including humorous portrayals of her personal story in books entitled, *Not Now…I'm Having a No Hair Day!*, *Our Family Has Cancer, Too!* (written especially for children), *Cancer Has Its Privileges: Stories of Hope & Laughter*, and *Laugh 'Til It Heals.*

Christine is currently president and chief executive officer of The Cancer Club®, a company designed to market humorous and helpful products for people who have cancer. She speaks to organizations worldwide about finding humor and getting through life's adversities.

She lives with her husband, Dan, in Bonita Springs, Florida and Minneapolis, Minnesota where she is a loving Grammy to two grandchildren.

Check out her websites at www.cancerclub.com and www.ChristineClifford.com. Don't forget to laugh!®

The Guardian Angel Feather ornament is available in either pink, teal, or blue. To order, visit us at www.cancerclub.com. A portion of each sale is donated to charity.